FATHERS UNDER GOD
A DEVOTIONAL FOR THE MEN WHO FORGE NATIONS

Building families strong enough to restore a nation

WRITTEN BY
ANDY THOMPSON
FOUNDERS OF SMORES AND STRIPES
CREATORS OF THE UNDER GOD PROJECT

Published by The Under God Project Press Dallas, Texas
© 2025 Andy Thompson. All rights reserved.

No portion of this publication may be reproduced or transmitted in any form or by any means without prior written permission of the publisher.

INTRODUCTION
WELCOME HOME AMERICA

"AS FOR ME AND MY HOUSE, WE WILL SERVE THE LORD."

—*JOSHUA 24:15*

INTRODUCTION

Men—this is not the hour to shrink back.

Our nation is starving for fathers, our homes are starving for leaders, and our children are starving for examples of strength rooted in love. The world will tell you that manhood is outdated, that drive fades with age, that strength is vanity, and that family is a burden. They are wrong.

God designed fathers to be the engine of legacy. When a man rises early, disciplines his body, embraces his wife, and blesses his children, something supernatural happens: strength multiplies, joy ignites, and covenant passes from one generation to the next.

This is not about muscles in the mirror. This is about muscle in the mission.
Testosterone is God's gift of drive, courage, and fight.
Oxytocin is God's gift of bonding, tenderness, and love.
When these two work together in a father, the result is unstoppable: a man who is steady, grounded, affectionate, and driven—what I call covenant strength.

That strength doesn't come by accident. It is forged in rhythm.
Morning: before the world wakes, you rise, train, and pray. You take the fight to gravity, to weakness, to complacency. You bend your body in discipline so your spirit is sharp for the day.

Evening: before the world sleeps, you bless your children, you laugh at the table, you hold your wife close, you bank the coals of covenant.

The Seventh Day: you march your family into the house of God. You declare publicly: "As for me and my house, we will serve the Lord."

These 7 lessons are not theory. They are weapons. They are levers God Himself built into your design—sleep, strength, food, peace, purpose, discipline, and rest. When you honor them, your body responds. When you practice them, your family thrives.
Brothers, this is the time to rise. Your children don't need a tired man. Your wife doesn't need a passive man. This world doesn't need another father on the sidelines. It needs men on fire—driven by covenant, fueled by joy, anchored in worship, and unshakable in strength.

This is your call. This is your training. This is your rhythm.
Now—pick it up. And run the race like a man who intends to win.

FATHERS CREED

I am a father Under God.
    I rise early to fight for my family.
    I discipline my body, so my spirit stays strong.
    I protect, provide, and pray without ceasing.
    I will laugh with my children,
    bless them by name,
    and lead them to worship the Lord.
    I will love my wife as Christ loves the Church.
    I will walk in covenant strength—
    joy in my heart, fire in my bones,
    and the Word of God on my lips.
    This is my calling.
    This is my mission.
    As for me and my house—we will serve the Lord.

OUR FAMILY UNDER GOD
AN AMERICAN FAMILY COMPACT

"As for me and my house, we will serve the Lord"

— JOSHUA 25:15

GOD MAKES FAMILIES

From the very beginning, God's design for nations began with fathers.

He did not start with armies, governments, or kings—He started with men who built homes.

When the floodwaters receded, Noah stepped out of the ark as a father and built an altar to the Lord, dedicating his household and the generations that would follow. When the world turned to idolatry, Abraham was called out of Ur to become the father of nations, leading by faith and obedience. When bondage held God's people captive, Moses led them out of Egypt as tribes and households—fathers leading families under God. When the promise passed to Isaac and Jacob, God renewed His covenant through their line, reminding them that their sons and their sons' sons would bear His Name.

God has always built nations through the faith and leadership of fathers.
Centuries later, that same truth echoes in America.

FATHERS UNDER GOD BUILT AMERICA

In 1954, President Dwight D. Eisenhower—himself a father and general—added the words "Under God" to the Pledge of Allegiance and signed it into law, affirming that our liberty flows not from government, but from our Creator. He did so because, for years, American fathers had already been leading their families to stand under God's authority.

In 1948, Louis Albert Bowman, a humble father from Chicago, first added "under God" to the Pledge at his church and family gatherings. Looking out at a world on the brink of war, he was inspired by Abraham Lincoln's timeless words from 1863—that "this nation, under God, shall have a new birth of freedom."

Lincoln's phrase at Gettysburg was not in his notes. He spoke it as a conviction—a father's cry for a nation's soul—echoing the divine truth proclaimed by the Founders in 1776: that all men are created equal and endowed by their Creator with unalienable rights—life, liberty, and the pursuit of happiness.

And those Founders, in turn, stood as fathers of faith upon the shoulders of those who came before them.
In 1620, my great-grandfather William Brewster helped pen the Mayflower Compact—the first governing document of this land. It was not written by prophet, pastor, president, or king, but by fathers. Fathers who knelt before God and declared that their colony would exist "for the glory of God and the advancement of the Christian faith."

FAMILIES MAKE NATIONS

THE COVENANT CONTINUES

From the Ark to the Mayflower, from Plymouth Rock to the halls of Congress, the story is the same:
When fathers remember God, families are strong and nations are preserved. When fathers forget Him, nations fall.

Every generation of fathers must renew this covenant in its time—inviting God back into our homes, our schools, and our national identity.

And so we return to Joshua, standing at Shechem after the battles were won. He called the people together, placed a great stone beneath the oak tree, and declared before all Israel:

"As for me and my house, we will serve the Lord." — JOSHUA 24:15

That stone stood as a witness to their covenant—a reminder that nations rise or fall on the faith of their fathers.

Today, this Compact is that stone. This is our covenant.

A LIVING COVENANT BETWEEN FAMILIES

Every Family Under God Compact is hand-pressed on archival paper, designed to last for generations. Each father signs his name, sealing his promise as the priest of his home—that his household will serve the Lord.

Fathers across the nation create their own family seals using the wax seal kit included in each Compact—a symbol bearing the words One Nation Under God. It is a declaration that their family is ordained and commissioned by God.

When these signed seals return to be included in future Compacts, each new father receives a tangible link to another man's covenant—a living reminder that we are truly One Family Under God.

Just as the Mayflower fathers united their families in a common promise, this covenant binds today's fathers together in a shared faith and destiny. It is a call to restoration—of home, of heritage, and of hope.

BOOK OF AMERICAN VIRTUES

AN AMERICAN FAMILY PROMISE

OUR FAMILY UNDER GOD

A Promise

We are the {...} family, and on this {...} day of {Month}, of, {year} we declare that we are One Family Under God.

We believe that it is our right and our privilege to glorify God, and to enjoy and give thanks for what He has given us, especially for one another. The story of our faith is a story of the creation, sanctification, and preservation of families, and the story of our family is a continuation of the divine story.

We believe that God created families, and therefore the family is sacred and ordained by God. We believe that our family was created specifically for this time.

We know that every father and mother before us has led directly to our family today, and we believe they have been placed in our history so that we could be brought together.

As a family we pledge to love one another, to be a light to each other and the world around us. We pledge to learn more about our family history, and to learn and instruct our children on how best to honor God with our time, our talents, and our treasures.

As parents, we believe that our children are a gift from God, and our highest responsibility on earth.

As children, we believe that we are given the opportunity to learn from our fathers and mothers, and theirs before them, how to live an abundant and fulfilling life by honoring God and our parents.

We believe we are always essential to each other, essential to God's family, our extended family on earth.

We know that though there may be prodigals, or in pain, or wandering for a time, and while some of us may have been lost, we are still a family created by God. All of us were once prodigals to God, yet never abandoned or lost to Him, so we commit to never abandon those he has given to us.

We pledge to strengthen our faith and family ties, to uplift and encourage one another, and to stand firm in the face of any effort within or without to dim our light, love, or liberty to one another.

To that end we promise together as a family to continually: {personal family promises}

May God give us patience, strength, and peace as we keep these promises to one another, and may

God bless
THIS AMERICAN FAMILY.
In the Name of God,
Amen.

FATHER LESSONS

Lesson 1 – Lifestyle Levers: Foundations of Strength
    Sleep as Obedience
    Strength Training as Stewardship
    Nutrition as Fuel
    Stress Management as Surrender
    Body Composition as Covenant Stewardship

Lesson 2 – Natural Boosters & Roadblocks
    Safe Natural Boosters: Creatine, Ashwagandha, Fenugreek, Tongkat Ali
    Roadblocks: Alcohol, Sugar, Chronic Cardio, Stress Mismanagement
    Stewardship, Not Shortcuts

Lesson 3 – Purpose, Covenant, and Family Energy
    Mission Fuels Testosterone
    Prayer Anchors Purpose
    Oxytocin + Testosterone Synergy in Family Bonding
    Covenant Clarity: As for me and my house, we will serve the Lord

Lesson 4 – The Biblical Backdrop for Strength
    Joy as Strength (Nehemiah 8:10)
    Covenant Multiplication (Ecclesiastes 4:9)
    Generational Training (Ephesians 6:4)
    The Body as Temple (1 Corinthians 6:19)

Lesson 5 – The Morning Watch: Strength and Discipline
    Rise Early with Purpose
    The Presidential Fitness Standard (50/50/50 + 5 Miles)
    Scripture Anchors for Training
    Covenant Renewal in Prayer

Lesson 6 – The Evening Sunset Rhythm: Bonding and Blessing
    Rest as Worship
    Bonding with Children: Eye Contact, Cuddles, Laughter, Prayer Covering
    Husband & Wife Connection
    Banking the Coals of Covenant

Lesson 7 – The Seventh Day: Rest and Worship
    Rest the Body, Restore the Spirit
    Lead Your Family to Church
    Family Worship at Home
    Joy as Strength, Worship as Legacy

LESSON 1

Lifestyle Levers Foundations of Strength

SCRIPTURE *Quote*

DEVOTIONAL 1

*"In vain you rise early and stay up late, toiling for food to eat—
for He grants sleep to those He loves."* — PSALM 127:2

Sleep is strength. It's the first discipline of trust—the rhythm God wove into creation to remind men that they are not machines, but image bearers.
When the Father rested on the seventh day, He wasn't weary—He was wise. He was teaching man that strength doesn't come from endless motion, but from sacred rhythm.

Before God brought Eve to Adam, He caused a deep sleep to fall upon him. Only in that stillness did God complete His work. Out of rest came relationship. Out of surrender came covenant. That moment still speaks: man's shoulders were never meant to carry the world, but to build it—with his Creator, and beside the helpmate God designed for him in eternity.

When you sleep, you join that same divine rhythm. God restores the muscles you've strained, balances the hormones that fuel your strength, and renews your mind for the mission ahead. Even one week of poor sleep can drop testosterone by 10–15%. That's not weakness—it's a warning. The body is crying out for what the soul has neglected: dependence.

Rest is readiness. Stillness is strategy. A father who sleeps well leads well. His patience lengthens, his focus sharpens, his presence deepens. His home finds safety in his calm, and his strength multiplies through trust.

Let darkness be your sanctuary. Let stillness be your strength.
Close your eyes not as a man retreating—but as a man obeying.
You were not made to carry the world—only to build it with Him.

Best conditions: a dark, cool room (65–68 °F), no screens an hour before bed.

SLEEP: STRENGTH BUILT IN STILLNESS

Father Reflection
Sleep is trust.
When you rest, you declare that God is on the throne even while you close your eyes. You're not giving up control—you're returning it to Him. The world runs on anxiety and ambition; fathers run on faith.
Your rest tonight becomes your family's refuge tomorrow.

Father Action
Audit: Record your bedtime and wake-up for seven nights. Average 7–9 hours.
Environment: Darken the room, lower the temp, and silence your phone.
Sabbath Preview: End each day by praying over your wife and children before lights-out.

Closing Prayer
Father, thank You for the gift of rest.
Teach me to trust You enough to sleep deeply and rise ready.
Quiet my mind, steady my breath, and let my dreams be guarded by Your peace.
Strengthen me through rest so I can lead my family in joy tomorrow.
Amen.

Where do I need to trust God enough to rest?

What worries keep me awake, and how can I surrender them in prayer tonight?

___

DEVOTIONAL 2

"PHYSICAL training is of some value, but godliness has value for all things."
— 1 TIMOTHY 4:8

Strength is stewardship.

It's not about image—it's about integrity. The body God gave you is the instrument through which your calling is played. Every muscle, joint, and heartbeat was designed to serve a mission far greater than appearance—to protect, provide, and lead with endurance.

When a man trains, he's not chasing vanity—he's tuning the instrument of his obedience. God gave Adam work before He gave him rest. He called him to subdue, cultivate, and multiply—a command that requires stamina. Strength is not optional in a man; it's essential to his design.

Physical training is worship in motion. Each rep, each mile, each breath that burns is an act of gratitude—a declaration that says, "This temple belongs to the Lord." Scripture reminds us, "Physical training is of some value, but godliness has value for all things." (1 Timothy 4:8) The two are not at odds—they are intertwined. Discipline of the body reinforces discipline of the spirit.

When you build your strength, you're preparing your life to lift others.
The stronger your shoulders, the safer your family feels beneath them.
The steadier your endurance, the calmer your leadership in storms.

Train not for applause, but for assignment.
Train not to be admired, but to be available.
Your body is a living covenant, declaring that you are ready to serve when God calls.

Every man must master gravity before he can carry glory.
So rise, move, and sweat with purpose.
Because every ounce of strength you build in discipline becomes fuel for love, joy, and legacy.

STRENGTH TRAINING

Father Reflection

Your children don't need a perfect body—they need a present father.

But presence takes endurance. A man who refuses to strengthen his body limits his legacy.

When you train, you're not chasing youth—you're honoring your calling.

Discipline in the gym becomes devotion in life.

Your sons will imitate your example. Your daughters will measure future men by your steadiness.

Father Action

Move Daily: Do at least one compound movement (pushups, pullups, squats, or deadlifts).

Train for Function: Focus on strength and stamina, not just appearance.

Pray While You Train: Let every rep become a rhythm of gratitude—"Lord, make me strong to serve."

Closing Prayer

Father, thank You for the body You have given me.

Make me a steward, not an idolater, of strength.

Let my training sharpen both muscle and spirit.

May every ounce of energy You restore in me become fuel to protect, provide, and lead with love.

Amen.

Where have I neglected my physical stewardship?

How can I invite God into my training—so my strength serves others, not myself?

DEVOTIONAL 3

"so whether you eat or drink or whatever you do, do it all for the glory of God."
— 1 CORINTHIANS 10:31

Food is fuel for the mission—not comfort for the flesh.
Every meal a man eats either strengthens his covenant or weakens his calling. God designed the body to be fueled by what He formed from the earth, not what man engineered in a lab. When you eat with purpose, you worship with discipline.

From the very beginning, God provided nourishment before He gave instruction. Adam was placed in a garden full of provision before being charged with purpose. What he consumed would either sustain his mission or sabotage it. The same is true for every father today—what you take in shapes what you can give out.

Nutrition is stewardship. The food you choose determines the strength you bring to your family. Protein rebuilds muscle. Healthy fats regulate hormones. Minerals like zinc, magnesium, and vitamin D fortify energy and endurance. These aren't fitness facts—they're faith tools. God embedded renewal into creation, waiting for men wise enough to honor it.

When you eat clean, you lead clear. When you overindulge, you dull your edge. The enemy wants men tired, foggy, and distracted. But a disciplined man—one who eats with gratitude and restraint—is sharp, alert, and ready for battle.

The dinner table is sacred ground. It's where your children learn what gratitude looks like, and where your wife feels the peace of your leadership. Every bite can become an act of praise, every meal a covenant of provision.

So eat like a man preparing for battle, not like one escaping from it.
Give thanks, eat with intention, and remember:
Fuel is more than food—it's faith in motion.

Guideline: Prioritize whole foods—protein, healthy fats, and minerals. Avoid processed sugars and gluttony. Eat to serve, not to soothe.

NUTRITION: FUEL FOR THE MISSION

Father Reflection

Fueling your body is fueling your family.
They eat what you eat, but more importantly—they live off the strength you either build or neglect.

When you choose discipline over indulgence, your children see that obedience is not deprivation—it's preparation.
When you thank God for what's on your plate, you remind them that provision is sacred.

The table is where strength begins—and legacy is served one meal at a time.

Father Action

Upgrade One Meal: Replace a carb-heavy plate with lean protein and healthy fats.
Hydrate Like a Leader: Drink water before coffee or energy drinks.
Bless Your Food: Pray aloud before every meal this week, even when you're alone.

Closing Prayer

Father, thank You for feeding my body and my soul.
Teach me to see food as fuel for faithfulness, not escape.
Help me eat and drink in ways that honor You and serve my family.
Let my strength, joy, and clarity become offerings of gratitude at Your table.
Amen.

How do my eating habits reflect my gratitude or neglect of God's provision?

Where do I need more discipline—and where do I need more grace?

DEVOTIONAL 4

"be still, and know that I am God."
— PSALM 46:10

True strength isn't just measured in muscle—it's revealed in peace.
A man may lift heavy in the gym and still collapse under the weight of worry. God never intended you to carry stress alone; He designed surrender as your pressure valve and prayer as your reset.

High cortisol—the body's stress hormone—drains testosterone, steals focus, and exhausts energy. Science calls it imbalance; Scripture calls it idolatry. It happens when a man starts trusting his own effort more than his Father's provision. Stress is a sign that you're trying to play God instead of following Him.

That's why the Bible commands, "Be still, and know that I am God." (Psalm 46:10) Stillness isn't passivity—it's power under control. It's choosing to pause before reacting, to pray before speaking, to breathe before breaking. In that moment of surrender, peace flows back in and strength resets.

A father who doesn't give his stress to God will give it to his family instead. But when he prays through pressure, his home becomes a refuge instead of a battlefield. His words soften. His shoulders lighten. His presence brings calm.

You are not built to grind endlessly; you are built to guard peace. Jesus Himself withdrew to quiet places—not to escape, but to equip. In your stillness, God restores your spirit and reorders your steps.

The man who masters peace becomes a pillar in his home. His wife trusts his steadiness. His children learn composure by his example. His spirit leads where fear once ruled.

Breathe. Release. Trust.
Every time you surrender stress, you strengthen your soul.

Practice: Step outside, breathe deeply, and hand your burdens to God aloud. Stillness is not weakness—it's the weapon that wins the war within.

STRESS MANAGEMENT

Father Reflection

A man who doesn't give his stress to God will give it to his family instead.
Prayer is the handoff.
Your wife doesn't need your rage—she needs your refuge.
Your children don't need your panic—they need your peace.
When you worship through pressure, you teach them where to turn when storms rise.
You model composure under fire—the kind only God can produce.

Father Action

Pause and Pray: When tension builds, stop. Take five slow breaths and invite God into that moment.
Go Outside: Ten minutes in sunlight resets your hormones and clears your thoughts.
Worship Over Worry: Replace complaints with gratitude out loud. It changes the atmosphere.

Closing Prayer

Father, I lay my burdens at Your feet.
Quiet my spirit, calm my mind, and steady my heart.
Teach me to surrender stress before it spills over onto those I love.
Make my peace a shield for my home and my faith a testimony to my children.
Amen.

What do I hold too tightly that belongs in God's hands?

Who absorbs the pressure I refuse to release?

DEVOTIONAL 5

"Do you not know that your bodies are temples of the Holy Spirit, who is in you, whom you have received from God? You are not your own."
— 1 CORINTHIANS 6:19

Body Composition: Covenant Stewardship

Your body is not a burden—it's a trust.
Every cell, every breath, every heartbeat was given to you on loan from God, to steward for His glory and your family's good. You were not built to worship your body, but neither were you called to neglect it. Stewardship means ownership under God's authority—a covenant between Creator and creation.

When Scripture says, "Your body is a temple of the Holy Spirit," it's not poetry—it's instruction. You are the sanctuary where God's presence and purpose dwell. A man's body reflects his discipline. Too much indulgence breeds weakness; too much apathy breeds decay. A strong temple requires care, order, and intention.

Excess body fat—especially around the midsection—does more than weigh you down. It alters your hormones, turning testosterone into estrogen, robbing energy, drive, and focus. But healthy balance restores vitality and vigor. When you fuel wisely and move consistently, your physical strength becomes a spiritual testimony—evidence that your covenant with God is active, not idle.

Covenant stewardship isn't about chasing perfection; it's about practicing obedience. The weight you refuse to lose becomes the burden your children carry—through fatigue, impatience, or disease. But when you care for your health, you extend your mission and model restraint to your family.

God didn't design men to chase vanity; He designed them to carry vision. Your health sustains that vision. The body is the engine of calling—maintained not by pride, but by purpose.

Discipline your body to serve your spirit.
Train your appetite to follow your mission.
Honor your temple, and your household will find refuge in your strength.

Practice: Eat with discipline, move daily, and measure progress by presence, not by pounds. A father's fit body is not pride—it's provision in motion.

BODY COMPOSITION

Father Reflection

The weight you refuse to lose becomes the burden your children carry. Every pound of discipline you shed today becomes an ounce of joy for them tomorrow.

You don't pursue fitness to look impressive—you pursue it to be dependable. When your family knows you are strong, they rest secure. When you choose health, you model hope.

Your body is a covenant tool—built for worship, work, and wonder.
Keep it ready for battle, blessing, and embrace.

Father Action

Move and Measure: Track progress not by weight, but by energy, consistency, and presence.
Cut the Sugar, Not the Joy: Replace empty calories with foods that give life, not steal it.
Use Accountability: Invite your wife or kids to join your health journey—make it family stewardship.

Closing Prayer

Father, thank You for this temple You have entrusted to me.
Forgive me where I have been careless, and strengthen me where I have been weak.
Teach me to honor You with my energy, my discipline, and my health.
Let my strength serve my household and reflect Your glory.
Amen.

What part of my health do I neglect most—and how does that affect those I love?

What would covenant stewardship of my body look like in this season?

LESSON 2:

Natural Boosters & Roadblocks

SCRIPTURE *Quote*

DEVOTIONAL 6

"better a patient man than a warrior, one with self-control than one who takes a city."
— proverbs 16:32

Stewardship, Not Shortcuts

Strength is never built through shortcuts—it's forged through stewardship. Every good thing God designed for a man's growth requires process. The soil must be turned before it yields fruit. The muscle must be tested before it gains power. The heart must be surrendered before it learns endurance.

Modern culture preaches instant gratification: fast gains, quick fixes, synthetic strength. But what the world calls progress, God calls pretense. The Father never blessed shortcuts—He blessed stewardship. His strength is found in rhythm, discipline, and faithfulness over time.

Supplements can serve a steward, but they can't save a sluggard. No pill can replace prayer, and no powder can replace purpose. True power is spiritual first, physical second. You can drink every booster and still be weak in character if your habits aren't anchored in holiness.

A man who chases shortcuts becomes dependent on what fades. But a man who walks with patience builds something that lasts. God's timeline strengthens both the body and the spirit. Every rep, every discipline, every quiet morning of training and prayer declares: "I'm not here for quick glory. I'm here for eternal impact."

The Father's calling is generational, not seasonal.
His strength must endure decades, not days.
And endurance is never sold in a bottle—it's built in obedience.

So steward what God has given. Move with intention. Eat with purpose. Train with consistency. Rest with faith.
That's how a man becomes unbreakable—inside and out.

Practice: Track consistency, not intensity. Measure success by habits sustained over time. A faithful steward may not move fast—but he will finish strong..

STEWARDSHIP NO SHORTCUTS

Father Reflection

There's no pill for purpose. No powder for perseverance. Your family doesn't need a man chasing edge—they need a man anchored in endurance.

Supplements can enhance a steward. But they can't replace a man who rises early, trains hard, eats well, and prays deeply.

Every shortcut comes with a tradeoff. The world sells speed; God rewards consistency.
Build slow. Build strong. Build sacred

Father Action

Assess Honestly: Take inventory of what you take—coffee, supplements, or stimulants. Why do you use them?
Reset Rhythm: Replace one artificial boost with a natural one—hydration, sunlight, deep sleep, or prayer.
Teach Legacy: Talk with your sons or friends about what real strength costs—and why it's worth the wait.

Closing Prayer

Father, guard my heart from chasing shortcuts.
Teach me to honor the long road—the one that builds endurance and faith.
Make my strength steady, not shallow; my discipline real, not rushed.
Let my stewardship reflect Your design, and my patience reveal Your glory.
Amen.

What "shortcut" tempts me most—physically or spiritually?

What would it look like to replace it with patient stewardship this week?

DEVOTIONAL 7

"The Lord God made all kinds of trees grow out of the ground—trees that were pleasing to the eye and good for food."
— GENESIS 2:9

Natural Boosters: God's Gifts of Creation

God placed everything a man needs for strength in the world He created.
From the dust of the ground He formed Adam—strong, clear-minded, whole. That same earth still holds the ingredients for renewal and endurance. What science calls "natural boosters," Scripture calls provision.

Long before laboratories and marketing, God wove His pharmacy into the fabric of creation. The sun for vitamin D. The sea for minerals. The soil for nourishment. Plants and roots—like Ashwagandha, Fenugreek, and Tongkat Ali—carry properties that balance hormones, lower stress, and restore vitality. These are not modern discoveries; they are ancient mercies—gifts hidden in plain sight for men wise enough to honor them.

But the purpose of these gifts is not replacement—it's reinforcement.
They were never meant to substitute obedience or discipline, but to support them. Supplements cannot restore what disobedience destroys. A man who won't sleep, eat, or pray with order cannot expect nature's benefits to override spiritual neglect.

Every booster is meant to remind you of the Giver, not replace Him.
When you use creation with gratitude, God blesses it. When you use it out of greed, it loses its power.

So receive creation as a covenant gift. Steward it with discernment. Let what grows from the ground strengthen the ground you stand on. Drink water as prayer. Take nourishment as worship. See every leaf, seed, and sunrise as proof that your Father still provides.

Practice: Before taking any supplement or booster, pause to give thanks. Ask God to use it for clarity, discipline, and endurance. Remember—the greatest booster a man will ever have is faithfulness.

NATURAL BOOSTER

Father Reflection

God built this world to help, not to harm, the men who walk it in faith.
When you approach creation with gratitude instead of greed, it responds with blessing instead of bondage.
Every plant, mineral, and nutrient is an echo of His care—a reminder that He provides the means to fulfill the mission.
Your role is to receive wisely and steward faithfully.

Be the kind of man who knows his body, honors his limits, and gives thanks for every natural advantage God offers.

Father Action

Evaluate: Research natural boosters prayerfully before using them. Seek wisdom, not hype.
Simplify: Add only what serves your rhythm—sleep, training, nutrition, and peace come first.
Steward: Keep your motives pure—strength to serve, not to show off.

Closing Prayer

Father, thank You for the gifts hidden in Your creation.
Teach me to use them with gratitude and discernment.
Let every supplement, every meal, every drop of strength remind me that You are my true source.
May my body serve Your mission, my mind stay humble, and my heart stay faithful.
Amen.

How can I honor God with the natural resources He's given?

Do I rely on His design—or chase the next "fix" the world sells me?

DEVOTIONAL 8

"Do not be deceived: God cannot be mocked. A man reaps what he sows."
— GALATIANS 6:7

Roadblocks: What Weakens a Man

For every good thing God provides to strengthen a man, the enemy offers a counterfeit to weaken him.

The devil doesn't always destroy men with obvious sins—he dulls them through slow, subtle indulgence. Alcohol numbs conviction. Sugar spikes energy, then crashes resolve. Laziness feeds guilt. Chronic stress erodes clarity. Before long, a man who was once sharp and strong begins to live in a fog—tired, reactive, and unanchored.

These are the roadblocks of strength. They don't announce themselves—they accumulate.
And every compromise carries a cost.
The drink meant to "take the edge off" soon takes away purpose.
The comfort food meant to soothe ends up stealing stamina.
The unchecked stress that feels productive turns the heart bitter and the home heavy.

God didn't design you to live dependent on what depletes you. He called you to discipline what distracts you. The man who learns to say no to the small things becomes trustworthy with the great things.

Every physical roadblock has a spiritual root: a hunger for control, escape, or comfort that only God can satisfy. The Father offers peace; the world offers coping. The difference is legacy.

You were built to lead from clarity, not chaos. Your body is a tool of worship, not a testing ground for indulgence.
A father who masters his appetites multiplies his influence. The one who yields to them loses it.

So strip away what drains you. Reject what dulls you.
The world tempts you to compromise—God calls you to conquer.

Practice: Identify one weakness this week—food, drink, distraction, or thought pattern. Fast from it for seven days. Let restraint rebuild your strength and obedience renew your joy.

ROADBLOCKS

Father Reflection

You don't lose strength overnight—you leak it. One compromise at a time. One "I'll start tomorrow" at a time.
But grace is stronger than habit.

When you surrender what drains you, God restores what defines you. Your body isn't just chemistry—it's covenant. Every good choice becomes an act of worship. Every refusal of compromise becomes an act of war.
You're not dieting—you're defending your destiny.

Father Action

Identify One Drain: Alcohol? Sugar? Chronic stress? Name it. Bring it to light.
Replace It: Swap a vice for a virtue—prayer walk instead of pouring a drink, cold water instead of soda, gratitude instead of anxiety.
Lead Out Loud: Tell your family what you're changing and why—make discipline visible.

Closing Prayer

Father, expose the habits that weaken me.
Remove from me the things that dull my purpose and drain my strength.
Replace craving with clarity, addiction with affection, exhaustion with energy.
Let my body be a testimony of Your renewing power,
and my discipline a light for my sons.
Amen.

What "roadblock" have I allowed to steal my strength?

What would repentance look like in action, not just intention?

___
___
___
___
___
___
___
___
___
___
___
___
___
___
___
___
___
___
___
___
___
___
___
___
___
___
___
___
___

LESSON 4

Purpose, Covenant, and Family Energy

SCRIPTURE Quote

DEVOTIONAL 9

Whatever you do, work heartily, as for the Lord and not for men."
— Colossians 3:23

Mission Fuels Testosterone

A man's strength was never meant to exist in isolation—it was designed to serve his mission.
Testosterone doesn't rise from comfort; it rises from calling. It thrives where there is purpose, direction, and a reason to fight for something eternal.

When God placed Adam in the garden, He didn't give him entertainment—He gave him assignment. "Work it and keep it." That divine mandate still fuels every man today. Mission gives meaning to muscle. It gives endurance to the ordinary and significance to the struggle.

Men lose their fire when they lose their why.
Drifting through days without direction lowers both passion and purpose. It's not just biology—it's theology. The Creator wired purpose into your design so deeply that your hormones respond to it. A man on mission walks taller, thinks clearer, and leads stronger because he knows who sent him and why he wakes.

Work becomes worship when it's done for the Lord. Whether you're building a company, raising children, or fixing a fence—your task becomes holy when your motive is heaven. The strength God placed in you is not for status; it's for service.

The man who walks in mission doesn't chase motivation—he cultivates momentum. Every task becomes training for legacy. Every challenge becomes confirmation that his calling still stands.

Your drive is divine. Your courage is chemical. Your strength is sacred.
Stay on mission, and your body, mind, and spirit will rise to meet it.

Practice: Write your mission in one sentence this week—your "why" as a father, husband, and man under God. Speak it aloud every morning before you begin your work. Let your purpose become your pulse.

MISSION FUELS TESTOSTERONE

Father Reflection

Men burn out when they forget why they burn. The answer isn't less effort—it's aligned effort.

When you work for legacy instead of applause, your strength multiplies. When you lead for covenant instead of comfort, your home becomes your headquarters.

Testosterone rises when purpose is clear because purpose gives your strength a name. Let your family see your work as worship. Let them know what you're fighting for.

Father Action

Define It: Write down your mission in one sentence—why do you rise each morning?
Align It: Bring your habits, health, and calendar under that purpose.
Declare It: Tell your wife and children your "why." Let them see you live it.

Closing Prayer

Father, thank You for giving me purpose beyond survival.
Ignite my drive with holy ambition.
Align my energy with Your mission and my strength with Your calling.
Let my work honor You, my leadership bless my family, and my purpose build legacy that lasts.
Amen.

If my sons copied my mission, would it lead them toward God or toward distraction?

Where am I wasting the energy God gave me for something greater?

_____
_____
_____
_____
_____
_____
_____
_____
_____
_____
_____
_____
_____
_____
_____
_____
_____
_____
_____
_____
_____
_____
_____
_____
_____
_____
_____
_____
_____
_____
_____

DEVOTIONAL 10

"COMMIT to the Lord whatever you do, and He will establish your plans."
— PROVERBS 16:3

Prayer Anchors Purpose

Prayer is not a pause in the mission—it's how the mission holds its course.
A man without prayer may move fast, but never straight. Prayer is what keeps power from drifting into pride and discipline from turning into self-dependence. It is the unseen anchor that keeps strength holy.

From the first breath of Adam to the last prayer of Jesus, the story of man has always been shaped by communion with the Father. When Jesus rose early to pray before the crowds gathered, He showed us that leadership without prayer is just noise. Every miracle He performed was rooted in a moment of stillness before God. Every victory began in surrender.

Prayer turns ambition into assignment. It converts drive into direction. It steadies the mind, humbles the ego, and aligns a man's energy with heaven's will. Without prayer, even noble work becomes noise—activity without anointing. But when a man prays, the smallest task becomes sacred ground.

A praying father builds clarity in chaos. His wife feels his steadiness. His children sense his peace. His work carries weight because it was born in worship.

Prayer is not for perfect men—it is for purposeful men. The ones who refuse to move without hearing orders from the Commander.

So make prayer your first act of war and your final act of rest.
Let your knees hit the ground before your hands hit the day.
Anchor your strength before you launch your mission.

Practice: Begin every morning with five minutes of prayerful silence—listening before speaking. End every day by releasing the day's burdens back to God. A man anchored in prayer never drifts far from purpose.

PRAYER ANCHORS PURPOSE

Father Reflection

Your strength means little if it's not surrendered. A father anchored in prayer can face storms that would sink stronger men.

When your children see you pray, they learn what it means to depend on Someone greater than dad. When your wife hears your prayers, she remembers that her husband leads with humility.

Prayer is not what you do after you fight—it's how you prepare to win.

Father Action

Start and End in Prayer: Begin each day with purpose; end each night in surrender.
Pray Aloud: Let your children hear your voice speaking to God—it becomes their model.
Pray Over Work: Before sending an email, making a deal, or starting a project, pause and dedicate it to the Lord.

Closing Prayer

Father, teach me to seek You before I strive.
 Anchor my goals in Your will and my actions in Your presence.
 Let every decision flow from devotion, not pride.
 Make me a man whose prayers build peace,
clarity, and strength for his home.
Amen.

Do my prayers shape my plans—or do my plans shape my prayers?

What would change if I invited God into the first five minutes of my day—every day?

DEVOTIONAL 11

"LET all that you do be done in love."
— 1 CORINTHIANS 16:14

Oxytocin + Testosterone: The Power of Family Bonding

God built both fire and gentleness into the heart of a man.
Testosterone fuels his courage, drive, and ambition. Oxytocin fuels his love, connection, and empathy. The world tries to separate them—making men either hard and distant or soft and aimless—but God designed them to work in covenant harmony.

From the beginning, man was made both warrior and worshiper. Adam was strong enough to guard the garden yet tender enough to name and nurture every living thing. In God's design, true masculinity isn't found in dominance—it's found in balance.

When you wrestle your son, your testosterone rises—but so does his trust.
When you hold your daughter close, oxytocin flows in both of you—building security and love.
When you pray with your family, both chemicals surge together—courage meeting compassion, strength meeting stillness.

God hardwired fatherhood to run on both power and peace. Testosterone without oxytocin produces aggression; oxytocin without testosterone produces passivity. But together, they form covenant energy—a man who can fight with conviction and love without fear.

Your family doesn't need a man who is merely strong; they need one who is safe. They don't need perfection; they need presence. Every hug, laugh, and word of blessing releases peace into your home.

When strength and tenderness meet, your family sees the face of the Father through you.
That's not biology—it's covenant chemistry.

Practice: Make physical affection and verbal affirmation part of your daily rhythm. Hug your children for at least 20 seconds. Speak blessing over them out loud. Let love be seen, felt, and heard.

OXYTOCIN + TESTOSTERONE

Father Reflection

A father without affection becomes a tyrant. A father without strength becomes fragile.
But a man who can wrestle his son and then whisper a prayer over him—that man changes generations.

Your family doesn't need perfection; they need presence. Every laugh, hug, and moment of calm builds safety in their souls. When your children feel your warmth, they understand God's heart. When your wife feels your embrace, she trusts your leadership. Bonding is not weakness—it's worship.

Father Action

Physical Bonding: Hug your wife and kids daily—long enough to mean it.
Play and Pray: Spend 10 minutes of joy-filled play before bed—then pray as a family.
Speak Love: Say the words out loud: "I'm proud of you." "I love you." "You make me happy."

Closing Prayer

Father, thank You for designing me to be both strong and gentle.
Teach me to lead with courage and love with compassion.
Let my words bring peace, my touch bring safety, and my presence bring joy.
May my family feel Your love through my strength and
see Your strength through my love.
Amen.

Do I balance strength and tenderness in my home—or do I lean too far one way?

How can I use both to reflect the heart of God to my family this week?

DEVOTIONAL 12

"but as for me and my house, we will serve the Lord."
— JOSHUA 24:15

Covenant Clarity: "As for Me and My House"

Every family follows something—culture, comfort, convenience, or conviction. But only one choice builds a legacy that lasts: serving the Lord together.

When Joshua declared, "As for me and my house, we will serve the Lord," he wasn't making a suggestion—he was drawing a line. He was claiming spiritual ownership of his home. That same clarity is what separates passive families from covenant families.

Covenant clarity is not about control; it's about commitment.
It's when a father decides that his home will not drift with culture but will anchor in truth. It's the declaration that the Word of God will be the standard for your household—above politics, pressure, and pride.

Every family reflects its leadership. If a father leads with conviction, his home carries peace. If he leads with confusion, his home carries chaos. The spiritual temperature of the family is set by the thermostat of the father's faith.

When you speak covenant over your home, you reclaim your authority as priest and protector.
You shift your posture from "What do we believe?" to "Who do we serve?"
Your children learn that faith isn't an accessory—it's identity.
Your wife feels covered by leadership that listens to God.

A house divided cannot stand. But a home united under God cannot fall.
The enemy can tempt, culture can pull, but covenant holds.

Practice: Gather your family this week and read Joshua 24:15 aloud together. Write it out or post it in your home where everyone can see it. Speak it often. Pray it daily. Let your household echo heaven's order: "As for me and my house, we will serve the Lord."

COVENANT CLARITY

Father Reflection

Men often chase titles that fade: CEO, coach, provider, leader. But the title Father Under God will echo for generations. Your covenant is not a contract—it's a commitment written in faith and sealed in love.

When you gather your family to worship, when you lead them to church, when you open the Word at home—you're declaring spiritual ownership. That declaration shifts the atmosphere of your home from survival to legacy.

It says: We belong to God. Our strength, our peace, our story—His.

Father Action

State It: Read Joshua 24:15 aloud with your family this week. Frame it or write it on your wall.
Live It: Dedicate one night a week to family worship, Scripture, or shared prayer.
Protect It: When the world pulls your family apart, remind them who you serve and why.

Closing Prayer

Father, thank You for entrusting me with a family and a mission.
Write Your covenant on the walls of our home and the hearts of my children.
Let our laughter be worship, our unity be testimony, and our service be legacy.
As for me and my house, we will serve You—today and every day.
Amen.

If someone spent a day in my home, would they know Who we serve?

What habits or rhythms can I build to make our covenant visible and unshakable?

LESSON 4

The Biblical Backdrop for Strength

SCRIPTURE *Quote*

DEVOTIONAL 13

"Do not grieve, for the joy of the Lord is your strength."
— NEHEMIAH 8:10

Strength isn't built only in sweat—it's built in spirit.
The Bible declares, "The joy of the Lord is your strength." (Nehemiah 8:10) That means your power doesn't come from adrenaline or achievement—it comes from abiding. True joy is not laughter without reason; it's peace without condition. It's the quiet confidence that God is good even when life is not.

A joyful man isn't naive—he's anchored. He doesn't ignore pain; he overcomes it by perspective. He doesn't lose himself in frustration; he lifts himself through faith. Joy transforms pressure into purpose. It's the fuel that keeps a father steady when the world shakes.

Science calls it emotional resilience. Scripture calls it worship.
When joy rises, stress falls. When gratitude fills the heart, hormones align and the body heals faster. Even biology bows to the truth that joy strengthens both spirit and flesh.

Joy is not passive—it's protective. It guards your marriage from cynicism, your home from heaviness, and your faith from fatigue. A man who leads with joy builds a house his family wants to come home to.

You can't manufacture joy, but you can magnify it. Worship stirs it. Gratitude feeds it. Fellowship protects it.
When your children see you laugh freely and praise loudly, they learn that joy is not weakness—it's worship in motion.

The world drains. God restores.
The joy of the Lord is more than a feeling—it's your Father's strength running through your soul.

Practice: Begin each morning with gratitude—three blessings spoken aloud. Joy grows where thankfulness is planted.

JOY AS STRENGTH

Father Reflection

A man without joy becomes a machine—efficient but empty. Your children don't remember how much you worked; they remember how much you smiled while you did it.

Laughter at the dinner table is a spiritual weapon. Gratitude before God in hard times is a declaration of trust.
 And a joyful man—steady, content, thankful—becomes a fortress for his home.

Your strength doesn't come from what you control; it comes from Who controls you.
 When the joy of the Lord fills your heart, even your presence heals.

Father Action

Start with Gratitude: Each morning, name three things that bring joy and thank God aloud for them.
Laugh Intentionally: Share a story, a joke, or a memory with your kids tonight.
Shift Your Atmosphere: When frustration rises, speak joy—sing, smile, or pray until your peace returns.

Closing Prayer

Father, fill me with the joy that no trial can steal.
 Teach me to smile in storms, laugh with my family, and praise You through pressure.
 Let Your joy be the strength that sustains my home
and the light that guides my children.
 In every challenge, remind me that joy is my inheritance and my weapon.
Amen.

When was the last time my children saw me laugh in faith instead of worry in fear?

What daily practice could protect my joy this week?

BOOK OF AMERICAN VIRTUES

DEVOTIONAL 14

"Two are better than one, because they have a good return for their labor."
— ECCLESIASTES 4:9

Covenant Multiplication

Strength multiplies in covenant.
When God said, "It is not good that man should be alone," He wasn't just talking about marriage—He was revealing the spiritual truth that no mission, no man, and no legacy stands in isolation. From the garden to the upper room, every move of God began in partnership.

Ecclesiastes 4:9 says, "Two are better than one, because they have a good return for their labor."
That's not mathematics—it's miracle. Covenant multiplies output, endurance, and impact. One man can chase a thousand, but two can chase ten thousand. (Deuteronomy 32:30) When men walk together under God's authority, their combined obedience unlocks exponential strength.

The lone wolf model of manhood is a lie. Isolation doesn't make you independent—it makes you ineffective. Accountability doesn't weaken you—it sharpens you. The father who walks with brothers in prayer and purpose carries more peace, more endurance, and more joy into his home.

Covenant multiplication starts in marriage. A husband and wife walking in unity become a fortress—one flesh, one mission, one faith. It extends into brotherhood, where men lock arms and hold each other to the standard of covenant living. And it grows generationally, as children learn that faith is a family effort, not a solo act.

Every time you pray with your wife, call a brother, or mentor a younger man, you multiply the kingdom through your strength.

God's economy runs on unity. His power flows through agreement. His legacy is written through family.

Practice: Pray with one person this week—your spouse, a brother, or a friend—and ask God to multiply strength through your unity. The miracle of covenant begins with connection.

COVENANT MULTIPLICATION

Father Reflection

Isolation drains men faster than sin. When you hide your struggle, you hand the enemy your silence.

But when you open your life to brotherhood—to another father who sharpens, prays, and checks in—your weakness becomes your weapon.

Your wife is your first covenant partner. Your brothers in Christ are your defenders on the wall.
 Your children are your multiplication in motion. Every relationship under God's authority becomes a force of legacy.

Father Action

Strengthen Your Circle: Text a brother today—ask how he's fighting, then pray for him.
Cover Your Wife: Pray over her out loud tonight. Let her hear strength in your voice.
Teach Your Kids: Show them what teamwork and covenant look like—include them in simple acts of service.

Closing Prayer

Father, thank You for the power of covenant.
 Surround me with brothers who sharpen me and family who strengthen me.
 Let my marriage, friendships, and fatherhood multiply Your legacy on the earth.
 Make me loyal, humble, and bold enough to walk with others toward Your call.
Amen.

Who are the men or family members I need to rejoin in covenant strength?

Where have I allowed isolation to weaken what God meant to multiply?

DEVOTIONAL 15

"FATHERS, do not provoke your children to anger, but bring them up in the discipline and instruction of the Lord."
— EPHESIANS 6:4

Generational Training

You are not raising children—you are raising legacy.
Every word, habit, and reaction in your home becomes the blueprint for how the next generation understands God, strength, and love.

Ephesians 6:4 says, "Fathers, do not provoke your children to anger, but bring them up in the discipline and instruction of the Lord." God isn't calling fathers to control their homes by force, but to lead them by formation. He calls us to shape—not to shame; to train—not to tear down.

The greatest sermon your children will ever hear isn't preached behind a pulpit—it's lived out at your dinner table. They will imitate your patience or your pride, your consistency or your compromise.
Every raised voice teaches something. Every apology does too.

Generational training begins in small moments—when you pray before meals, when you pause before reacting, when you open Scripture together, when you say "I was wrong." These are lessons of legacy, teaching your sons to be humble warriors and your daughters to trust godly strength.

A father's job is not to make his children behave—it's to make them believe.
Believe that love is safe. That truth is real. That faith works.
You are not building perfection—you're building direction.

Raise them to know God's Word, not just your rules.
Discipline them with purpose, not frustration.
And lead them with a heart anchored in grace, because the way you handle their weakness will teach them how to handle yours.

Practice: Choose one moment each day this week to teach intentionally—a verse, a story, a prayer, or a correction done in love. Legacy isn't built in lectures—it's built in moments of faithfulness.

GENERATIONAL TRAINING

Father Reflection
Your home is a training ground, not a battlefield. Every moment—at breakfast, in the car, during chores—is a classroom.

You are not raising children; you are raising future fathers and mothers, husbands and wives, leaders and servants of God. They will copy your tone, your patience, your discipline, and your prayers.

The greatest sermon they'll ever hear is the one you live daily—faithful, steady, and rooted in grace.

If you want your children to love the Lord, let them see how much you do.

Father Action
Teach with Patience: Correct your children calmly, explaining the "why," not just enforcing the "what."
Model First: Let them catch you reading Scripture, praying, or apologizing when you fall short.
Train Daily: Give them small missions—chores, prayers, or acts of service—to grow their strength and purpose.

Closing Prayer
Father, thank You for trusting me with the souls of my children.
Teach me to discipline with love, to guide with grace, and to lead by example.
Let my home be a place of peace, growth, and godly training.
May my words plant truth, my actions model faith, and my legacy reflect You.
Amen.

What habits am I training into my children—intentionally or unintentionally?

What do I want my sons and daughters to remember about how I led our home?

DEVOTIONAL 16

"Do you not know that your bodies are temples of the Holy Spirit, who is in you, whom you have received from God? You are not your own; you were bought at a price. Therefore, honor God with your bodies."
— 1 Corinthians 6:19–20

The Body as Temple

Your body is not your own—it's a temple.
God designed you to carry His presence, not just His purpose. Every heartbeat, every breath, every act of discipline is sacred because the Spirit of God lives within you.

1 Corinthians 6:19–20 says, "Do you not know that your bodies are temples of the Holy Spirit, who is in you, whom you have received from God? You are not your own; you were bought at a price. Therefore, honor God with your bodies."

This means strength, purity, and health are not personal projects—they're acts of worship.
You don't work out to impress; you train to serve.
You don't eat clean to look better; you do it to live ready.
You don't pursue fitness to chase youth; you pursue discipline to chase faithfulness.

Your body is the vessel through which your calling flows. A tired, neglected temple limits your influence. But a disciplined, rested, nourished body multiplies your capacity to love, lead, and endure.

This truth reaches beyond the physical—it's spiritual.
A man who guards his health often guards his holiness.
When you treat your body with reverence, you teach your family that worship doesn't end at church—it continues in how we live.

Your children learn stewardship by watching how you move, eat, and rest.
Your wife feels your care when she sees your consistency.
Your home benefits when your temple is strong.

So honor what God has entrusted to you.
Train it. Feed it. Rest it.
Your strength is His stage—let it reflect His glory.

Practice: Before every workout or meal, say this simple prayer: "Lord, let my body honor You today." A temple maintained in worship becomes a vessel of power.

THE BODY AS TEMPLE

Father Reflection
Your family lives in the overflow of how you treat your temple. When you're healthy, they inherit your energy.
When you're disciplined, they inherit your stability. When you're pure, they inherit your peace.

The Holy Spirit doesn't just visit you on Sunday—He resides in you every moment. Your stewardship of the body is part of your stewardship of the Spirit. When your children see you care for yourself without vanity, they learn that faith touches everything.

Your body is not an idol—it's an instrument of praise.

Father Action
Move as Worship: Train or walk today with prayer on your lips. Let sweat become song.
Clean the Temple: Remove one unhealthy habit from your week—replace it with prayer or fasting.
Teach It: Tell your children why health matters to God. Connect fitness to faith.

Closing Prayer
Father, thank You for making my body a temple of Your Spirit.
Forgive me where I've treated it carelessly or pridefully.
Teach me to move, eat, and rest as a man entrusted with Your presence.
Let my strength become service, and my health become worship.
Amen.

If my body is God's temple, what part of it have I neglected to honor?

What habits could transform my strength into a daily act of worship?

LESSON 5

The Morning Watch

SCRIPTURE *Quote*

DEVOTIONAL 17

"very early in the morning, while it was still dark, Jesus got up, left the house and went off to a solitary place, where He prayed."
— MARK 1:35

Rise Early with Purpose

Purpose begins before sunrise.
The first hour of your day determines the tone of your life. Long before the world demands your attention, heaven waits for your devotion.

"Very early in the morning, while it was still dark, Jesus got up, left the house, and went to a solitary place, where He prayed." (Mark 1:35)
Jesus modeled what every father must master—the discipline of meeting the day before it meets you. Rising early isn't about productivity; it's about priority. It's saying to your Creator, "You lead; I'll follow."

Morning is the furnace of strength. It's when the mind is sharp, the spirit is quiet, and the body is most responsive. When you rise with purpose, you claim dominion over your time instead of letting the world dictate it. You silence chaos before it begins.

Men who wake early don't just get more done—they become more grounded.
The man who meets God before sunrise carries a different spirit into his work and family. His confidence comes from communion, not caffeine. His strength flows from structure, not stress.

In that solitude, God speaks. He reveals direction. He sharpens conviction.
A man who wins the morning will win his marriage, his fatherhood, and his mission.

Your alarm clock isn't an interruption—it's an invitation.
The day is waiting for leadership. Your family is waiting for order.
The world is waiting for men who move with divine intention.

Practice: Set your alarm 30 minutes earlier this week. Spend that time in Scripture, prayer, or physical training before the noise begins. Win the first hour, and the rest will follow.

RISE EARLY WITH PURPOSE

Father Reflection
The alarm clock is not your enemy—it's your invitation. Each sunrise whispers: You have another chance to lead well. When your children see you rise early to pray or train, they see what priority looks like. They see that leadership starts before the world calls and before excuses form.

Your wife feels safer when she wakes to a man already moving with purpose. Your spirit stays sharper when your first victory is over comfort.

Rise early—not for pride, but for preparation. The day will follow the father.

Father Action
Start with Stillness: Before checking your phone, sit or kneel in silence. Thank God for breath and purpose.
Train the Temple: Move your body—walk, stretch, or lift—before the day's demands take over.
Set the Tone: Speak a blessing aloud over your home before anyone else is awake.

Closing Prayer
Father, thank You for the gift of morning.
Teach me to rise with focus, strength, and gratitude.
Let my early hours be filled with Your presence and
my actions reflect Your purpose.
May my day follow Your rhythm and my family follow my example.
Amen.

How does my morning routine reflect my priorities?

If my children copied my first hour of the day, would they rise stronger—or slower?

DEVOTIONAL 18

*"Do you not know that in a race all the runners run, but only one receives the prize?
Run in such a way as to get the prize."*
— 1 CORINTHIANS 9:24

The Presidential Fitness Standard: Training the Temple

Strength is not about competition—it's about commitment.
Every man was designed to train his body in order to train his character. The same discipline that pushes through a workout pushes through adversity. The same focus that finishes a set finishes a calling.

Paul writes, "Do you not know that in a race all the runners run, but only one receives the prize? Run in such a way as to get the prize." (1 Corinthians 9:24)
He wasn't just talking about athletics—he was teaching endurance.
A father's race is lifelong, and the prize is generational legacy.

The old Presidential Fitness Standard—50 pushups, 50 sit-ups, 50 squats, and a 5-mile run—wasn't just a test of endurance; it was a statement of readiness. It told a nation, "Strength matters." God says the same to His men today. When you train your body, you are declaring, "I'm prepared to serve."

Training doesn't glorify you—it equips you. A strong body protects your family, fuels your mission, and stabilizes your emotions. A disciplined man becomes dependable. And dependability is a spiritual quality.

The goal is not perfection, but progression.
A man who improves his physical condition is also improving his spiritual capacity. Every drop of sweat becomes a sacrifice of praise. Every step forward says, "I'm ready for the weight of responsibility."

So train the temple. Move the body God gave you.
Let every repetition remind you that strength and stewardship are the same call.

Practice: Choose one benchmark this week—pushups, squats, or distance—and improve it daily. Not to prove strength, but to prepare for service. A father fit for his purpose blesses generations.

PRESIDENTIAL FITNESS STANDARD

Father Reflection

Strength fades when comfort rules. A lazy body soon teaches a lazy faith.

But a man who pushes his limits daily trains more than muscle—he trains mission. When your children see you sweat with joy, they learn that effort is sacred. When your wife sees your consistency, she feels your covering.

You don't have to be the strongest man in the room—just the most faithful one in your lane. A father in motion keeps his family in motion.

Father Action

Set the Standard: Begin with 10 pushups, 10 squats, 10 sit-ups, or 1 mile—then grow from there.
Consistency Over Perfection: Move daily, even briefly. The habit matters more than the record.
Train Together: Invite your children to join you. Let laughter and sweat blend into worship.

Closing Prayer

Father, thank You for this body and the strength to move it.
Train my will as much as my muscles.
Let my daily discipline shape my family's future and reflect Your endurance in me.
May I run the race to win—not for pride, but for purpose.
Amen.

Do I treat my fitness as worship or as a chore?

What standard could I set this month that challenges me and inspires my family?

DEVOTIONAL 19

"Your word is a lamp to my feet and a light to my path."
— PSALM 119:105

Scripture Anchors for Training
Strength begins in Scripture.
The body may lift the weight, but the Word lifts the man. Without truth, even the strongest father drifts. Without Scripture, even the most disciplined body becomes directionless.

"Your word is a lamp to my feet and a light to my path." (Psalm 119:105)
That means every workout, every task, every test of endurance must begin in light—anchored in truth that steadies the mind and sanctifies the mission.

The gym builds muscle; Scripture builds meaning.
You can push through pain, but only the Word teaches purpose. You can train for an hour, but only the Word transforms a life. Physical endurance must be tethered to spiritual obedience, or it becomes vanity disguised as virtue.

When a man trains his body with the Word in his heart, every rep becomes worship. Each breath reminds him of divine breath—the Spirit that fills his lungs.
Each step echoes creation's rhythm—ordered, intentional, holy.

The Word keeps your effort from drifting into ego.
It redirects the grind into gratitude. It replaces performance with perspective.
When you lift, run, or train with Scripture in mind, your strength no longer points to you—it points to the One who sustains you.

A father anchored in Scripture trains differently. He doesn't move for attention—he moves for alignment. His children see devotion in motion. His endurance becomes inheritance.

Let the Bible be your playlist. Let truth set your tempo.
Before every lift, every jog, every challenge, open the Word and let it lead the way.

Practice: Write one verse on a notecard or tape it to your training space this week. Read it before you move. Sweat under Scripture, and your body will follow your spirit.

SCRIPTURE ANCHORS FOR TRAINING

Father Reflection

God's Word is not meant to be skimmed—it's meant to be sweated through. Let it breathe into your lungs and pulse through your veins.

Imagine starting every workout with a verse, not a playlist. You're not chasing personal records; you're chasing spiritual readiness. And as you strengthen your body, Scripture strengthens your mind.

When your children see your Bible open next to your dumbbells, they'll learn that true power begins on your knees.

Father Action

Verse of the Day: Choose one Scripture before every training session. Meditate on it as you move.
Pray Between Sets: Turn rest periods into reflections—thank God for endurance and direction.
Post the Word: Write a verse near your weights, mirror, or running route as a reminder of purpose.

Closing Prayer

Father, thank You for the living Word that sharpens both spirit and strength.
Anchor my discipline in Your truth and keep my training aligned with Your will.
Let every step, lift, and breath declare that my power comes from You alone.
May my body move with faith and my heart stay anchored in Your Word.
Amen.

What Scriptures stir my strength or renew my focus?

How can I integrate the Word into my physical routine this week?

DEVOTIONAL 20

"THOSE who wait on the Lord shall renew their strength; they shall mount up with wings like eagles, they shall run and not be weary, they shall walk and not faint."
— ISAIAH 40:31

Covenant Renewal in Prayer

Every dawn deserves a declaration.
Each morning, a father must re-sign the covenant that defines his strength. Not with ink, but with prayer—with breath, with focus, with surrender.

"Those who wait on the Lord shall renew their strength; they shall mount up with wings like eagles; they shall run and not be weary, they shall walk and not faint." (Isaiah 40:31)

Prayer is not passive—it's preparation. It's the hinge between strength and purpose, where effort meets endurance. The man who trains but doesn't pray builds muscle without mission. The man who prays renews both.

Morning prayer is covenant renewal—it's how a father remembers who he is and Whose he is. It's not about fancy words; it's about faithful posture.
When you bow before the day, you rise with authority.
When you hand your burdens to God before they form, you walk lighter.
When you ask for wisdom before decisions arise, you move with confidence.

Prayer in the morning does what no caffeine can—it aligns chemistry with calling. Cortisol lowers, testosterone steadies, and peace floods the mind. You become anchored, aware, and armed for the day's battles.

Every sunrise is God's invitation to recommit.
To say again: "As for me and my house, we will serve the Lord."
To live again as a man under oath—strong in body, steady in spirit, surrendered in heart.

The day belongs to whoever claims it first. Claim yours on your knees.

Practice: Before you train, drive, or check your phone, kneel for two minutes. Pray aloud: "Lord, renew my strength, reestablish my covenant, and let today glorify You." A father anchored in prayer begins every day unshakable.

COVENANT RENEWAL IN PRAYER

Father Reflection

A man who begins his day with prayer walks differently through it. His mind stays anchored, his words stay measured, his reactions stay holy.

When you finish training and lift your hands to heaven, sweat becomes incense and strength becomes offering. Your children may not understand what you're doing—but they'll feel the peace it brings into your home.

Covenant renewal isn't about repeating words—it's about remembering the relationship. Each morning says again: As for me and my house, we will serve the Lord.

Father Action

Pray After You Train: End every workout or morning devotion by thanking God for the gift of strength and the day ahead.
Speak Blessing: Pray aloud for your wife and children by name—before they wake if possible.
Recommit Daily: Declare your covenant: "Lord, my strength is Yours. My family is Yours. My mission is Yours."

Closing Prayer

Father, I renew my covenant with You this morning.
You are my strength, my stability, and my song.
Let my prayers rise like the morning sun, warming my home with Your peace.
I offer You this body, this day, and this mission—
again and again—until the work is done.
Amen.

How can I make prayer the seal of every morning, not the afterthought?

What does covenant renewal look like in my daily rhythm?

LESSON 6

The Evening Sunset Rhythm

SCRIPTURE *Quote*

DEVOTIONAL 21

"Come to Me, all you who are weary and burdened, and I will give you rest."
— MATTHEW 11:28

Rest as Worship

Rest is not weakness—it's worship.
It's the moment a man stops striving and starts trusting.
The world glorifies exhaustion, but the Kingdom honors rhythm. God Himself worked six days, then rested—not because He needed recovery, but because He wanted remembrance. He set the seventh day apart so His sons would know: creation is complete, provision is enough, and control belongs to Him.

"Come to Me, all you who are weary and burdened, and I will give you rest." (Matthew 11:28)
Jesus didn't invite men to collapse; He invited them to commune. True rest doesn't come from inactivity—it comes from intimacy.

When a father ends his day in worship, peace fills his home.
He's not checking out—he's checking in. He's acknowledging that his strength has limits and his God does not. Rest becomes the bridge between stewardship and surrender, between duty and delight.

Your body repairs, your mind resets, and your spirit recovers while you sleep—but more importantly, your faith renews. Rest is trust made visible. It's saying, "God, I'm not holding this night together—You are."

A man who can rest in peace will rise in power.
His wife feels the calm of his spirit.
His children sense safety in his stillness.
And heaven takes pleasure in a man who knows when to work and when to worship.

Practice: Set an evening ritual of rest—dim lights, pray aloud with your family, and speak gratitude over the day. Let your last act before sleep be surrender. In doing so, you teach your home that rest isn't quitting—it's crowning the King.

REST AS WORSHIP

Father Reflection

The way you end your day preaches louder than how you start it. A man who rushes to bed in exhaustion teaches his children that rest is escape. A man who ends the day in peace teaches them that rest is reverence.

When you close your eyes with prayer instead of worry, you lead your home into calm. When you give your exhaustion to God, you wake with renewed strength instead of residue. The quiet of evening is not a void—it's a sanctuary.

Father Action

Create a Nightly Ritual: Dim lights, pray with your family, and speak gratitude before sleep.
End the Noise: No screens an hour before bed—invite stillness, not stimulation.
Rest with Intention: As you lie down, say aloud, "God, You reign. I rest."

Closing Prayer

Father, thank You for the rhythm of evening.
Teach me to rest in Your strength, not my own striving.
Quiet my thoughts, slow my heartbeat, and let Your peace cover my home.
May my rest become worship, and my stillness a song of trust.
Amen.

Do I treat rest as recovery or as worship?

What could I change tonight to end my day in peace instead of pressure?

___

BOOK OF AMERICAN VIRTUES

DEVOTIONAL 22

"He will turn the hearts of the fathers to their children, and the hearts of the children to their fathers."
— MALACHI 4:6

Bonding with Children: Eye Contact, Laughter, and Prayer Covering
The heart of a child is built on connection.
A father's love shapes identity, and his presence builds peace. Every look, laugh, and prayer exchanged between a father and his children becomes mortar in the foundation of trust they will stand on for life.

"He will turn the hearts of the fathers to their children, and the hearts of the children to their fathers." (Malachi 4:6)
This verse isn't about sentiment—it's about revival. When fathers turn their hearts homeward, nations heal. When fathers reengage with their children, homes stabilize and generations remember what love feels like.

Bonding is not an event—it's a rhythm.
When you kneel to listen, when you laugh without hurry, when you lay a hand on your child's head and pray, you are shaping eternity in ten quiet minutes. These small moments do what lectures and punishments never can—they teach worth, belonging, and safety.

A child who ends their day seen, loved, and covered in prayer grows up confident in who they are and secure in Whose they are.
Your voice becomes the soundtrack of their peace.
Your laughter becomes the echo of God's joy.
Your prayers become the shield around their dreams.

You don't need to be perfect—you need to be present.
The heart of fatherhood isn't authority—it's availability.

Practice: Each night, make eye contact with each child. Speak one word of affirmation, share one moment of laughter, and end with a personal prayer over them by name. Your blessing tonight becomes their courage tomorrow.

BONDING WITH CHILDREN

Father Reflection

Your kids won't remember every gift—but they'll remember your gaze. They won't remember every correction—but they'll remember your laughter. And they'll never forget the sound of their name lifted in prayer.

Bonding with your children isn't a sentimental act—it's spiritual warfare. When you connect, you guard their hearts from isolation and fear. When you bless them, you reinforce heaven's claim over their identity. You are not just ending their day—you are shaping their destiny.

Father Action

Look and Listen: Give each child five undistracted minutes of full attention tonight.
Laugh Together: Tell a story, play a short game, or share a joke—joy invites safety.
Pray by Name: Lay a hand on each child and pray a blessing specific to their day.

Closing Prayer

Father, thank You for the gift of my children.
Turn my heart fully toward them as You turn theirs toward me.
Let my eyes, words, and laughter reflect Your love.
Cover their dreams with peace and their futures with favor.
May our evenings become holy ground where covenant grows stronger.
Amen.

Do my children feel seen, safe, and spiritually covered at the end of each day?

How can I turn bedtime into a sacred family ritual of bonding and blessing?

DEVOTIONAL 23

"Therefore what God has joined together, let no one separate."
— MARK 10:9

Husband & Wife Connection: Banking the Coals of Covenant
Marriage is not maintained by momentum—it's sustained by intention.
Love cools where connection stops. A wise husband learns to bank the coals of his marriage each night, keeping warmth alive until morning.

Jesus said, "Therefore what God has joined together, let no one separate." (Mark 10:9) That's not a wedding verse—it's a command to preserve what God Himself designed. Covenant isn't kept by ceremony—it's kept by daily choice. Every night offers a new chance to strengthen the bond, to replace tension with tenderness, and to cover the day with grace.

Banking the coals of covenant means protecting what burns beneath the surface—respect, affection, laughter, prayer. It's the quiet moment when you choose unity over pride and gratitude over grievance. A gentle word before sleep repairs what harsh words may have wounded.

A strong marriage doesn't need grand gestures; it needs steady ones.
Touch her hand.
Thank her for her work.
Pray with her, not just for her.
Let her feel that she is your first ministry, not your last responsibility.

When a wife feels seen, she feels safe.
When she feels safe, she trusts.
And when she trusts, the entire home rests in peace.

You are not just loving your wife—you're leading your legacy.

Practice: Before bed, connect intentionally—one minute of eye contact, one word of affirmation, one prayer of blessing. End each night with warmth, not withdrawal. The coals you bank in covenant tonight will ignite tomorrow's joy.

HUSBAND AND WIFE

Father Reflection
The atmosphere of your marriage sets the tone for your home. Children thrive when affection flows freely between their parents. They rest easier when the covenant is strong.

Your wife doesn't just need your protection—she needs your pursuit. She needs to know she is still your first ministry, your first affection, and your first earthly covenant.

When you love her well, you love your children better. And when the two of you walk in unity, the Spirit of God dwells richly in your home.

Father Action
Connect Before Sleep: Hold her hand or embrace her for 30 seconds in silence. Let peace settle between you.
Speak Life: End the day with one affirmation—"I'm grateful for you," or "You make our home beautiful."
Pray Together: Cover your marriage aloud before bed. Ask God to guard your covenant and refresh your unity.

Closing Prayer
Father, thank You for the gift of my wife and the covenant You created between us.
Forgive me for every moment I've taken her for granted.
Teach me to love her as Christ loves the Church—with strength, patience, and grace.
Let our laughter echo Your joy and our unity reflect Your glory.
May our marriage be the warm fire that lights our children's world.
Amen.

Have I been pursuing my wife as passionately as I pursue my work or my goals?

What habit could I start tonight to keep the coals of our covenant burning bright?

DEVOTIONAL 24

"THE Lord bless you and keep you; the Lord make His face shine on you and be gracious to you; the Lord turn His face toward you and give you peace."
— NUMBERS 6:24–26

The Evening Blessing: Banking the Coals of Covenant at Home
Every home ends the day in one of two ways—exhausted or blessed.
One collapses under chaos; the other closes in covenant. A father's final words each night can shift the atmosphere from noise to peace, from worry to worship.

"The Lord bless you and keep you; the Lord make His face shine on you and be gracious to you; the Lord turn His face toward you and give you peace." (Numbers 6:24–26)

These words were given to Aaron, the first priest of Israel, but their spirit now rests on every father who leads under God. You are the priest of your home. Your blessing carries weight in heaven.

To "bank the coals of covenant" means to preserve warmth—to guard unity, gratitude, and grace in the quiet hours before morning. A gentle word, a shared prayer, or a simple "I love you" seals the day in strength. It says, "This house belongs to the Lord."

You don't have to end the day with perfection—end it with peace.
Your children need your calm more than your correction.
Your wife needs your presence more than your performance.

When you speak blessing over your home, you remind darkness that it doesn't dwell here. You invite the Prince of Peace to reign through the night.

A father's final duty is not to finish every task, but to fill every heart with assurance: we are loved, we are safe, and God is near.

Practice: Each night, walk your home softly. Thank God for what He provided, forgive what went wrong, and bless every room in prayer. You are the keeper of the coals—guard the peace that keeps your covenant alive.

THE EVENING BLESSING

Father Reflection
The world teaches men to collapse at the end of the day. God teaches fathers to consecrate it. When you walk your house in gratitude, when you pray over each room, when you speak peace aloud—you shift the spiritual temperature. Your tone sets the climate. Your words set the weather. You are the keeper of the coals—the one who ensures the warmth of covenant never goes out in the night.

Father Action
Bless Your Household: Pray a short blessing aloud over your home before bed—"Lord, keep our hearts united and our rest protected."
Walk the Perimeter: Silently thank God for each family member, room, and responsibility.
Leave the Light of Peace: End the evening with calm conversation or Scripture reading instead of screens or stress.

Closing Prayer
Father, thank You for the sacred rhythm of evening.
Tonight, I bless my home, my wife, and my children in Your name.
May peace rest on these walls, warmth linger in our hearts,
and faith carry into the morning.
Let the coals of covenant burn steady through every night
until the dawn You bring.
Amen.

What kind of atmosphere do I create in my home each night—one of exhaustion or one of peace?

What blessing can I begin speaking consistently over my family?

LESSON 7

The Seventh Day, Rest and Worship

SCRIPTURE *Quote*

DEVOTIONAL 25

*"THEN God blessed the seventh day and made it holy,
because on it He rested from all the work of creating that He had done."*
— GENESIS 2:3

Rest the Body, Restore the Spirit

Rest is God's idea, not man's invention.
It's built into the blueprint of creation—a commandment, not a suggestion. "Then God blessed the seventh day and made it holy, because on it He rested from all the work of creating that He had done." (Genesis 2:3)

Before sin entered the world, God established Sabbath. That means rest is not a response to brokenness—it's part of holiness. It's how a man declares, "I trust the God who holds my world together more than my effort to hold it myself."

The Sabbath is not laziness—it's loyalty. It's the day a man steps back to remember that provision doesn't come from performance, but from Presence. When you rest, you proclaim that God is the Provider and you are the steward.

Your body is strengthened through work, but your spirit is renewed through worship. Both are required for balance. Without rest, your strength becomes stress; without worship, your rest becomes apathy. The father who learns to pause in God's rhythm finds greater endurance in his calling and greater peace in his home.

Rest resets perspective. It reminds your children that achievement isn't identity. It restores joy to your marriage and quiets the noise of the world.

Honor the seventh day as God did. Shut the door to striving. Open the door to gratitude.
Rest is not an interruption—it's instruction.

Practice: Choose one day this week to rest fully—no work, no distractions, no guilt. Spend it in worship, gratitude, and joy with your family. The world won't fall apart when you rest—but it might start to heal when you do.

REST THE BODY, RESTORE THE SPIRIT

Father Reflection

A man who never stops working forgets Who his Provider is.
When you rest, you teach your children that God—not effort—sustains your home.

The Sabbath isn't just for sleep; it's for seeing again—seeing your wife, your kids, your blessings, and your purpose.
It's a reset of gratitude and grace.

Your rest is leadership.
It says to your family, "We trust Him enough to stop."
It says to your flesh, "You are not the master."

Father Action

Mark the Sabbath: Choose one day a week for rest, worship, and family focus.

Cease Striving: Avoid unnecessary work, screens, or tasks that drain your peace.

Restore Joy: Do something that brings life—a walk, a meal, or shared laughter with your family.

Closing Prayer

Father, thank You for teaching me the rhythm of rest.
Help me slow down and see Your goodness.
Restore my body, renew my spirit, and refresh my family through Your peace.
Teach me to trust You enough to stop—and to worship You through stillness.
Amen.

Do I see rest as obedience or as indulgence?
What practical boundaries could I set to protect sacred rest each week?

DEVOTIONAL 26

"I was glad when they said unto me, 'Let us go into the house of the Lord.'"
— PSALM 122:1

Family Worship at Home
The truest altar in your life isn't in a church—it's in your home.
Every meal prayed over, every Scripture spoken, every song sung in your living room is worship. When a father leads his family in praise and prayer, the presence of God takes residence there.

"These commandments that I give you today are to be on your hearts. Impress them on your children. Talk about them when you sit at home and when you walk along the road, when you lie down and when you get up." (Deuteronomy 6:6–7)

Faith is not inherited—it's demonstrated.
Your children will remember what you modeled long after they forget what you said. A father who prays with his family teaches more about God than a thousand sermons could.

Family worship doesn't have to be formal—it has to be faithful.
Read one verse after dinner. Thank God aloud before bed. Sing, even if off-key. Talk about what you're grateful for. These small rhythms become sacred traditions. They build spiritual muscle memory in your children, teaching them that worship isn't confined to a pew—it's lived out in the home.

When fathers bring Scripture into conversation and prayer into daily life, homes become sanctuaries. Peace fills the air. Joy rises. Arguments fade. Worship realigns the heart of the family with the heart of God.

You are your children's first pastor and your home their first church.
When you lead them in worship, heaven listens.

Practice: Choose one night each week for family worship. Read one passage, share one truth, and pray together by name. The family that worships together learns to weather anything together.

LEAD YOUR FAMILY TO CHURCH

Father Reflection

Church is not just a service; it's a statement. When your children see you stand, sing, and pray, they learn what leadership under God looks like. When your wife sees you lift your hands, she feels safe following your lead.

You are the spiritual thermostat of your household. If you burn bright, they will warm beside you.

If your fire fades, so will theirs. The next generation's faith begins with a father's footsteps to the altar.

Father Action

Prepare Together: Help your family get ready for church calmly—set the tone before you arrive.

Lead by Example: Sing, pray, and listen actively during service. Let your children see your engagement.

Talk Afterward: Discuss what you learned and how it applies to the week ahead. Make faith conversation normal.

Closing Prayer

Father, thank You for the house of worship.

Let my steps toward Your sanctuary be steady and joyful.

Teach me to lead my family with humility, consistency, and courage.

May our attendance be more than habit—may it be heritage.

Let every Sunday renew our covenant with You and with one another.

Amen.

How do I model excitement about worship for my family?

What could I do this Sunday to make church the highlight—not the afterthought—of our week?

DEVOTIONAL 27

"THESE commandments that I give you today are to be on your hearts. Impress them on your children. Talk about them when you sit at home and when you walk along the road, when you lie down and when you get up."

— DEUTERONOMY 6:6–7

Family Worship at Home

The truest altar in your life isn't in a church—it's in your home.
Every meal prayed over, every Scripture spoken, every song sung in your living room is worship. When a father leads his family in praise and prayer, the presence of God takes residence there.

"These commandments that I give you today are to be on your hearts. Impress them on your children. Talk about them when you sit at home and when you walk along the road, when you lie down and when you get up." (Deuteronomy 6:6–7)

Faith is not inherited—it's demonstrated.
Your children will remember what you modeled long after they forget what you said. A father who prays with his family teaches more about God than a thousand sermons could.

Family worship doesn't have to be formal—it has to be faithful.
Read one verse after dinner. Thank God aloud before bed. Sing, even if off-key. Talk about what you're grateful for. These small rhythms become sacred traditions. They build spiritual muscle memory in your children, teaching them that worship isn't confined to a pew—it's lived out in the home.

When fathers bring Scripture into conversation and prayer into daily life, homes become sanctuaries. Peace fills the air. Joy rises. Arguments fade. Worship realigns the heart of the family with the heart of God.

You are your children's first pastor and your home their first church.
When you lead them in worship, heaven listens.

Practice: Choose one night each week for family worship. Read one passage, share one truth, and pray together by name. The family that worships together learns to weather anything together.

FAMILY WORSHIP AT HOME

Father Reflection

Your home is the first church your children will ever attend. You are their first pastor, their first example, their first shepherd.

When they see you open the Word, they learn reverence. When they hear you pray, they learn trust. When they watch you sing, they learn joy.

A father who worships at home builds walls of peace and foundations of faith. The Spirit fills the space where the father leads in surrender. You don't need perfection—you just need presence.

Father Action

Set a Rhythm: Choose one time each day or week for family worship—morning, mealtime, or bedtime.
Include Everyone: Let each family member read, pray, or share what they're thankful for.
Keep It Joyful: Let laughter and authenticity flow. The goal is connection, not performance.

Closing Prayer

Father, thank You for making my home a sanctuary of Your presence.
Teach me to lead worship with joy, humility, and consistency.
Fill our table, our laughter, and our rest with Your Spirit.
Let every corner of this home echo with praise and
every heart grow stronger in faith.
Amen.

Does my home reflect worship between Sundays?

What simple habit could we start this week to make our house a house of praise?

DEVOTIONAL 28

"ONE generation shall commend Your works to another, and shall declare Your mighty acts."
— PSALM 145:4

Joy as Strength, Worship as Legacy

Worship is not a performance—it's inheritance.
When you lift your hands in gratitude, your children learn how to lift theirs.
When they hear your voice sing, they discover what hope sounds like.
When they see your joy in the Lord, they begin to understand what strength really is.

"One generation shall commend Your works to another, and shall declare Your mighty acts." (Psalm 145:4)
Worship isn't just about you—it's about the generations watching you. Your joy in God becomes the memory they carry into their own storms. It's how faith travels from father to son, from mother to daughter, from home to history.

The enemy works to drain joy because he knows it's the fuel of legacy.
A bitter father raises anxious children; a joyful father raises courageous ones. Joy doesn't come from ease—it comes from assurance. It's knowing that God is still good, even when life feels hard. It's the quiet strength that refuses to bow to fear or fatigue.

When your home echoes with laughter, thanksgiving, and praise, the Spirit inhabits those sounds. Joy becomes the rhythm of resilience. Worship becomes the anthem of endurance. Generations are strengthened not by wealth or comfort, but by the memory of seeing their father rejoice in the Lord.

Your strength builds a home.
Your worship builds a heritage.
Your joy builds a nation.

Practice: End this week with a song. Gather your family, thank God aloud for His faithfulness, and let joy fill your home.
Because when fathers worship, legacies awaken—and America's story continues, one household under God.

WORSHIP AS LEGACY

Father Reflection
Fathers shape legacies not by how loudly they lead, but by how faithfully they worship. When your kids hear your voice sing, even off-key, they know God is real. When they watch you bow your head in reverence, they see humility that commands respect. When they witness your joy in the Lord, they feel safe in His love.

Worship builds spiritual muscle. Joy keeps it flexible. Together, they preserve the rhythm of covenant for generations to come. Your life is your family's worship service—and your joy is their invitation to join it.

Father Action
Model Worship: Sing or pray aloud this week where your children can see and hear you.
Share the Story: Tell them one testimony of God's goodness from your own life.
Protect Joy: End each Sabbath with gratitude and laughter—let them remember the peace that followed worship.

Closing Prayer
Father, thank You for the gift of joy and the calling of worship.
Let my praise become the pattern that shapes my children's faith.
Fill our home with songs of gratitude and stories of Your faithfulness.
May our joy be unshakable, our worship unending, and our legacy everlasting—
as one family under God.
Amen.

What do I want my children and grandchildren to remember about my worship?

How can I make joy in the Lord the legacy my family carries forward?

FATHERS BENEDICTION

Declaration

I am a father under God.
I was not made for comfort but for covenant. I rise early to fight for my family and rest humbly in the arms of my Creator.

My body is a temple. My words are weapons. My home is an altar.

I will train my hands for work and my heart for worship. I will love my wife as Christ loves the Church. I will bless my children by name and lead them to know the Lord.

I will pull the levers of strength God designed—sleep, food, discipline, and peace— not for vanity, but for victory.
Not for applause, but for legacy.

My joy will not depend on circumstance. My strength will not fade with age. Because the same Spirit that raised Christ from the dead lives in me.

Blessing

May your mornings burn with purpose. May your evenings rest in peace. May your body be steady, your mind clear, and your heart full of joy.

May your sons see your courage and rise to carry it further. May your daughters feel your love and know the heart of their Father in heaven. May your wife walk beside you in unity, laughter, and grace.

And when your days are done— May your name still whisper faith. May your legacy still point to Jesus.
And may your family stand strong under the banner:
"As for me and my house, we will serve the Lord."

Closing Prayer
   Father of all strength,
   Thank You for the sacred calling of manhood, fatherhood, and covenant.
   Let every lesson I've learned and every habit I've built draw me closer to You.
   Bless my home with protection, my heart with perseverance, and my lineage with light.

   May my life—however brief—leave a mark of faith that endures forever.
   In the name of Jesus Christ, the perfect Son and the model of all fathers,
   Amen.

www.ingramcontent.com/pod-product-compliance
Lightning Source LLC
Chambersburg PA
CBHW051325110526
44582CB00004B/100